Text Analytics with Python

A Brief Introduction to
Text Analytics with Python

By Anthony S. Williams

owned by the owners themselves, not affiliated with this document.

Table of Contents

Introduction

Text analytics or text mining is all about deriving some high-quality structured data from obtained unstructured data. A very good reason for using text analytics might be extracting some additional data about customers from obtained unstructured data sources, in order to enrich that customer master data and to produce entirely new customer insight as well as to determine sentiment about different services and products. The most common text analytics applications are in case of management, for instance, healthcare patient record and insurance claims assessment. Text analytics is widely used as well in competitor analysis, media coverage analysis, sentiment analytics, voice of the customer, pharmaceutical drug trial improvement, fault management and different fields of service optimization.

Text mining or text analytics is a certain process of converting obtained unstructured data into some meaningful data notably used for further analysis especially when it comes to the measuring customer opinions, feedback and product reviews in order to provide search facility, entity modeling, and sentimental analysis in order to support mainly fact-based decision making. Text mining uses techniques from several different fields including machine learning techniques, statistical and linguistic techniques. Text mining also involves different information particularly retrieved from unstructured data as well as the process of properly interpreting that output data in order to derive trends and patterns as well as to evaluate and interpret the output data.

Text mining commonly involves categorization, lexical analysis, pattern recognition, annotation, clustering, tagging, visualization, information extraction, predictive analytics and association analysis. This certain field of data analytics provides different tools, algorithm-based applications, extraction tools and servers used for converting unstructured data into some meaningful data notably used for further analysis. The outputs of such data analytics are some extracted entities and facts particularly with certain relationships stored in some relational XML or some other warehousing applications by various tools like big data analytics, predictive analytics or business intelligence tools.

Text mining is commonly referred to as text mining notably equivalent to text analytics. As I already mentioned it is the process of deriving some high-quality as well as relevant and useful information from various textual data. This high-quality information is commonly derived through a certain process of devising various patterns and different trends through various means like statistical pattern learning. Text analytics commonly involves the certain process of structuring different input data like parsing in addition to some already derived linguistic features as well as the removal of some other features. Further text analytics involves certain driving patterns within that structured data and eventually evaluation as well as interpretation of the certain output data.

That high-quality feature in text analytics refers to a certain combination of novelty or relevance. Common text analytics task includes text clustering, text categorization, entity extraction, document summarization, production of different granular taxonomies, entity relation modeling and sentiment analysis. This process also commonly involves lexical analysis and information retrieval when it comes to the studying word distribution and frequency, annotation and tagging, information extraction. When it comes to the overall goal of text analytics process, it is to turn some text into structured data prepared for analysis via different applications, mainly natural language processing, and different analytical techniques.

A typical text analytics application is to scan a certain collection of documents specifically written in some natural language. The following step is to model that scanned document collection for further predictive classification purposes as well as to populate that database or search index so it contains all of the information previously extracted.

Text Analytics is a certain field of data analytics commonly used in scientific papers, different business intelligence spheres and many other scientific fields regarding big data analytics. Once the text has been obtained, text analytics software engaged a certain number of different text analytics system, which aims to answer three broad questions. So, using text analytics software you can find who is talking and what are they discussing and saying and how they feel. This is very useful when it comes to the customer feedback, product, and service reviews.

Text Analytics:

- Sentiment Analysis

- Summarization

- Visualization

- Text Identification

- Text Clustering

- Search Access

- Entity or Relation Modeling

- Link Analysis

- Text Mining

- Text Categorization

Commonly, the term text analytics is used in order to describe a collection of different statistical, linguistic and machine learning techniques, which structure and model the information or different textual source for exploratory data analysis, investigation, research and business intelligence. The term is very similar to text mining. However, the term text mining is mainly used in different business settings. This term also commonly describes which application or different text analytics applications respond to certain business problems both independently and in conjunction with some query and numerical data.

It should be noted that eighty percent of various business-relevant information, in fact, originates from unstructured data, mainly text. These text analytics techniques, as well as process, are used in order to discover and later present knowledge including business rules, facts and relationships notably locked in that textual from specifically impenetrable without text analytics to automated processing. We are witnesses to increasing interest in text analytics especially in recent times since multilingual data mining techniques can easily gain information across different languages as well as cluster some similar items from various linguistic sources in accordance with their meaning. Therefore, there is no surprise in the fact that text analytics has grown to be among the most important big data analytics techniques.

Chapter 1 Text Analytics Process

When it comes to the great challenges of exploiting that large proportion of enterprise information, which originates mainly from some unstructured form it has been recognized for decades now. These challenges are recognized in the business intelligence earliest definition back in 1958 in a journal article written by H.P. Luhn.

In his article, Luhn described a business intelligence system as a system used for utilizing different data-processing machines for auto-encoding and auto-abstracting of different documents in order to create some interesting profiles for every action point within a single organization. He also added that both internally and incoming generated documents are further automatically characterized and abstracted by a certain word pattern notably sent automatically to some proper action points.

Certain management information systems have been developed in the 1960s. At this time, IBM has emerged in the 90s as a particular software category as well as a certain field of practice notably emphasizing the importance of numerical data commonly stored in some relational databases. This was not surprising at all since text within some unstructured documents is a very challenging task to be processed easily.

The emergence of different text analytics techniques in this current form greatly stems from refocusing data analytics research, which took place back in the 1990s from algorithm development to different applications.

The fact is that for almost a decade the certain computational linguistics community simply has viewed amazingly large text collection as a certain resource notably used for tapping to produce some better quality and more useful text analytics algorithms. Later, the new emphasis on the text analysis has been introduced especially when it comes to the usage of different large online text data collection in order to discover some new trends and facts about the world we live in and about our future.

Search   **Big Data**

Text
Analytics

Text analytics task starts by generating different semantics in order to bridge big data and search. Text analytics applications enable different next-generation information systems. Semantic search includes obtained textual data while being mainly based on different text analytics applications. On the other hand, big data provides access to valuable and relevant information used for text analytics.

Subtasks or common text analytics process include information retrieval, natural language processing, named entity recognition, identification of certain noun phrases, sentiment analysis, quantitative text analysis and relationship, event or fact. The process of information retrieval is commonly referred to as identification of obtained corpus as an initial or preparatory step in the process of text analytics. The process includes collecting and identifying a certain collection of different textual materials commonly held in some file system or on the Web database.

There are some text analytics systems notably applying some exclusively advanced statistical methods. However, the most common methods applied in the text analytics process is natural language processing like syntactic parsing, speech tagging and other types of different linguistic analytics methods. Text analytics process commonly involves named entity recognition specifically using gazetteers and different statistical techniques in order to identify different named text features like place names, organizations, stock ticker symbols, people and various abbreviations. Disambiguation is also commonly involved in text analytics process including the use of different contextual clues notably required in order to make certain decisions.

The following step involved in text analytics process is recognition of different pattern identified entities. For instance, different features like telephone numbers, various quantities with units or e-mail addresses may be discerned using pattern matches and some other regular expressions. The next step commonly involved is coreference. It is the process of identifying different noun phases as well as other terms, which commonly refer to the exact same object. Event, relationship or fact extraction is the process of identifying different associations existing among different entities. Relationship extraction is also used when it comes to the identifying other information contained in obtained textual data.

Sentiment analysis is mandatory text analytics task notably commonly involving discerning subjective material as well as extracting different forms of some attitudinal information like emotion, mood, opinion, and sentiment. Text analytics techniques are very helpful when it comes to the analyzing various sentiments within an entity and distinguishing various opinion holders. Another commonly used task in text analytics techniques is quantitative text analysis notably representing a certain collection of different techniques stemming from some social sciences. Quantitative text analysis can give us answers to questions regarding a human judge involved in different computer extracts semantic. Quantitative text analysis also is very helpful when it comes to finding grammatical relationships between various words to find the stylistic patterns and meaning of commonly some casual personal text used for psychological profiling.

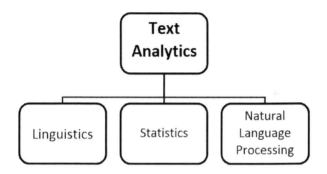

Text analytics techniques are widely applied to different spheres of business and research needs including scientific discovery including life sciences, enterprise business intelligence, competitive intelligence and data mining, e-discovery, national security, records management, sentiment analysis tools or listening platforms, publishing, social media monitoring, automated and placement, information search and information access.

Many text analytics software packages are commonly marketed for different security applications especially when it comes to the monitoring as well as analyzing some online text source like Internet news and other mainly for national security purposes. Text analytics techniques are also commonly involved in the study of text decryption and encryption.

A wide range of text analytics applications are used in biomedical text mining. On the other hand, text analytics techniques and software are commonly used as well as developed by some major companies like Microsoft and IBM in order to further automate the text analysis process. These different companies working in this field greatly contribute to improving the overall text analytics results. It is more than apparent that public sector is greatly concentrated on creating certain software notably used for monitoring and tracking some against the law activities, so text analytics has been of great help.

Text analytics methods have a wide range of online media applications used by some major companies like Tribune Company. In this specific scientific field, text analytics methods are used in order to provide readers with better search experiences that commonly increase site revenue and interestingness. Major media houses are focused on assembling and organizing their content while using faster and better semantic publishing provided by common text analytics methods. On the other hand, major editors are commonly benefiting by being capable of sharing, associating and packaging news across various properties notably greatly increasing their opportunities when it comes to the monetizing their content.

Majority of text analytics techniques and methods is starting to be used in business and marketing applications especially when it comes to the customer relationship management. Major business and marketing companies apply text analytics techniques in order to attract customers and keep their attention. Text analytics methods are also commonly used when it comes to the stock return prediction.

When it comes to the sentiment analysis, its techniques and methods are commonly used in an analysis of various movie reviews in order to estimate how favorable a certain review is for a specific movie. This kind of text analysis commonly requires some labeled data collection as well as affectivity of different words. When it comes to the certain resources for affectivity of words, analytics commonly use ConceptNet and WordNet software. Text commonly has been used in order to detect various emotions in some related are of commonly used affective computing. Text-based techniques and approaches to various affective computing methods have been used when it comes to the news stories, children stories, and student evaluations.

We are witnesses of huge amounts of text contained on Web and other file containers commonly used by big data analytics. That certain text online is creating vast relevant and useful data about many things like what is happening in the world or what different people think. All of this relevant data is an absolutely invaluable resource which can be mined in order to generate very useful business insights for organizations and analysts. However, in order to analyze all of this obtained content is very challenging, since converting that obtained text mainly produced by people and arranging it into some structure information in order to analyze it with a certain machine is a very complex task.

In recent years, text analytics methods and natural language processing have become a lot more useful and accessible for every data scientist, developer, and data analyst. Today, you have that huge amount of available resources, APIs, code libraries and various services that are of great importance on your journey towards creating your first natural language processing project. In order to make it easier, text analytics project in Python will be divided into several steps, so you will better understand the overall text analytics process. You will start from scratch while being introduced to very common code libraries and APIs for every task including building a corpus, analyzing text and visualizing your results.

The step of building a corpus will be executed using Tweepy in order to gather some sample data from common Twitter's API notably used in our project for text analytics purposes. The next step includes analyzing the certain sentiment or piece of text using SDK, commonly used software development kit. The last step includes visualizing results where you will get to know how to use Pandas as well as matplotlib in order to see the final results of your project.

Building a Corpus

You are able to build your own corpus easily from everywhere if you have that large collection of e-mails that you want to analyze. You may have a collection of various customer feedbacks obtained in some surveys and you want to dive into them. On the other hand, you maybe want to devote to the voice of online customers. There are many options entirely opened to you, but in the following section, we will use some Twitter posts as a focus of our corpus. Twitter is very useful when it comes to the amazing source of different textual content since it is easily accessible as well as the public. It also offers an insight into an amazingly huge volume of text, which contains worldwide public opinion. In order to start you have to access the Twitter Search API, and doing so in Python is not that challenging. There are many libraries available to anyone, but we will use Tweepy. We will use this certain library in order to ask the Twitter for the most recent Tweets, which contain your specific search term. The following step is to write the results in a text file and each Tweet will be represented on its very own line. This will make it very easy to analyze different Tweets entirely separately in the following step. In order to begin, you will install Tweepy via pip. As soon as the installation is over, you will open Python.

```
pip install tweepy

import tweepy
```

It should be noted that you would need a permission from Twitter in order to gather the most recent Tweets. In order to do so, you will sign into Twitter as a developer in order to access tokens and get your customer keys. This process will not take long, only about three to four minutes. The following step is to build search query while adding the certain search term to that query field. You will also add some additional parameters like the amount of results you need, language, and the certain time period for search. You can get very specific about what information you need and what you need to search.

```
import the libraries

import tweepy, codecs

consumer _ key = 'your consumer key here'

consumer _ secret = 'your consumer secret key here'

access _ token = 'your access token here'

access _ token _ secret = 'your access token secret here'

auth = tweepy . OAuthHandler (consumer _ key, consumer
_ secret)

auth . set _ access _ token (access _ token, access _ token _
secret)

api = tweepy . API (auth)

results = api . search(q = "your search term here", lang =
"en", result_type = "recent", count = 1000)

file = codecs . open ("your text file name here.txt", "w",
"utf-8")

file . write (result . text) file . write ("\n")

file . close ()
```

The first step is to import libraries and fill in certain Twitter credentials. Then, you will let Tweepy set up a certain instance of the API and then you will fill your search query as well as store results in a certain variable. The following step is to use the codecs library in order to write the certain text of the obtained Tweets and covert it to text format. You will see that the script containing certain writing results will not be that simple API notably returning to you. In this scenario, APIs commonly return certain language data form various social media as well as from online journalism sites lots of various metadata in addition to your results. In order to do this, APIs commonly format their outputs in an easy machine to read, JSON.

In your script, every result will have its own JSON object containing text notably just a single field containing the Tweet text. When it comes to the other fields in that certain JSON file, they will contain metadata such as the timestamp or location of the certain Tweet that you easily can extract in order to get more detailed text analysis. In order to access the rest of metadata, you will need to write a JSON file. On the other hand, if you want to the full list containing JSON files, you will have to print everything and return API back to you.

Analyzing Sentiment

The following step once you collected certain text within Tweets is to analyze every single obtained Tweet. In order to start, you may use some more advanced natural language processing tools. In this certain case, we will use sentiment analysis that is very useful whether you need to obtain some positive and negative opinions or some neutral sentiment in the text you have obtained. In order to perform sentiment analysis, you will use your own AYLEIN Text API just as you used Twitter Search API. In order to begin, you have to sign up for that free plan in order to grab your API key. In this case, free means you will get that key for free permanently. This certain free plan will give you thousand calls to the API per every month entirely free of charge. In order to start, you will install using pip again, just like in the previous step.

pip install aylien - apiclient

from aylienapiclient import textapi

As soon as you get your API key, you will return your JSON results back to your metadata just as you did with that Twitter API. In order to analyze your corpus from the previous step, you have to analyze every single Tweet separately. This will give you the text containing all the Tweets predicted by your AYLIEN API. You are able to look through your file in order to verify the results as well as to visualize them to see more metrics regarding people's feelings about your search query.


```
from aylienapiclient import textapi

import csv, io

client = textapi . Client ("your _ app_ID", "your _ app _ key")

io . open ('Trump_Tweets.csv', 'w', encoding='utf8', newline='')

csv _ writer = csv . writer ( csvfile )

csv _ writer ( "Tweet", " Sentiment" )

io . open ( "Trump.txt", 'r', encoding='utf8' )

f . readlines ()

tweet = tweet . strip ()

len (tweet) = = 0: print ( 'skipped' )

print ( tweet )

sentiment = client . Sentiment ({ 'text': tweet })

csv _ writer . writerow ([ sentiment[ 'text' ], sentiment [' polarity ']])
```

The first step is to initialize that new client of your AYLIEN Text API. Then, you will remove those extra spaces that are empty so you will not waste your API credits. You will make a call to your AYLIEN Text API and write your sentiment results into csv file.

Visualizing Your Results

The next step involves visualizing your results. So far you have used an API in order to obtain that text from Twitter and you used your Text Analysis API in order to analyze what people's opinion on a different subject is whether positive or negative in their Tweets. At this certain point, you have several options regarding what you may do with your final results. You may feed that structured information about various sentiments into some solution you are building that could be anything from an automated report to some simple social listening application. It also may be the public reaction to a certain public campaign.

You may use the obtained information in order to build some very informative visualization, and in this section, we will do just that. You will use matplotlib in order to visualize your data. You will also use Pandas in order to read your csv file. We will use this Python library since they are very easy to get up and running. You will create visualization directly from the command line and save it as a png file.

```
pip install matplotlib

pip install pandas

import matplotlib . pyplot as plt

import pandas as pd

from collections import Counter

import

df = pd . read _ csv( csvfile )

sent = df [ "Sentiment" ]

counter = Counter ( sent )

positive = counter [ 'positive' ]

negative = counter [ 'negative' ]

neutral = counter[ 'neutral' ]

labels = 'Positive', 'Negative', 'Neutral'

sizes = [ positive, negative, neutral ]

colors = [ 'green', 'red', 'grey' ]

yourtext = "Your Search Query from Step 2"

plt . pie (sizes, labels = labels, colors = colors, shadow =
True, startangle = 90)

plt . title ( "Sentiment of Tweets about "+ yourtext )

plt . show ()
```

You will notice that script below will open your csv file and then it will use Pandas in order to read that column titled as sentiment. It will also use Counter feature in order to count how many times every sentiment appears. Further, matplotlib will plot certain Counter's results to some color-coded pie chart. For this step, you will have to use your text query variable mainly for presentation reasons. The first step when it comes to the visualizing your results is to import two Python libraries. Then, you will open your csv file containing the sentiment results.

Further, you will use Counter in order to count how many times a certain sentiment appears and then you will save every variable. The following step is to declare the variable in order to use them in a pie chart. In order to do so, you will use the Counter variables for different sizes. In order to plot the chart, you will use matplotlib. If you want to save your chart instead of just showing it, you will replace a part show command on that last line with another command save fig that will contain the name of your pie chart.

Chapter 2 Named Entity Extraction

Named entity extraction is the process of recognizing different named entities by identifying variously named text figures commonly including places, products, people, brands, and organizations. However, named entity extraction may also be configured to anything your organization may require like specific abbreviations, certain strains of the disease, trading stocks and almost everything else notably tagged and identified as an entity. Text analytics methods commonly identify different pattern-based entities like phone numbers, e-mail addresses, and street addresses.

In the following section of the book, you will see how to build your own named entity recognizer using Python. It is the first step on your journey towards information extraction from obtained unstructured data. It means extracting what is a real world person, organization or some other entity. You will need to map it against some knowledge base in order to understand what the certain sentence is all about. You will also need to extract certain relationships existing between different named entities. In this certain situation, we will use Python's NLTK library since it contains a standard named entity annotator, so you can get started quickly.

```
from nltk import word _ tokenize, pos _ tag, ne _ chunk

sentence = "John and Lisa are working at Google."

print ne _ chunk (pos _ tag (word _ tokenize (sentence)))

""" (S (PERSON John/NNP) and/CC (PERSON
Lisa/NNP) are /VBP working/ VBG at /IN
(ORGANIZATION Google/NNP) ./.) """
```

This ne chink function will need part-of-speech annotations in order to add certain NE labels to specific sentences. It will further act as a chunker. It means that is produced two-level tress including nodes on the first level and nodes on the second level. Nodes within the first level are outside of that chunk while nodes on the second level are within that chunk so the bales will be denoted by that certain sub-tree.

It is very likely that for every question, there is written the answer somewhere, so you want to extract relevant and valuable information from text. It should be noted that the amount of valuable natural language text is completely astonishing and all if it is available in certain electronic form. This amount is also increasing every day. However, this great complexity of natural language can easily make it very challenging to access that information in some certain text. The state of the art when it comes to the natural language processing is still a long way from being something easily achievable and far away from being able to build those general-purposes representations of some meaning obtained from unstructured text. However, if we focus our efforts on that limited set of questions also knows as certain entity relationships we are able to significantly progress.

Groningen Meaning Bank Corpus

Named entity extraction is all about recognizing different means of unstructured data while identifying text figures including places, people, organizations, street addresses and almost everything else notably in textual form. For processing valuable information in Python, it is great to use IOB tagging that comes very useful for extracting those needed information notably used for text analytics purposes. It should be noted that IOB tagging is not that standard way of chunks since it will contain a certain initial word contained in the chunk, all words within the chunk as well as all the words outside of the chunk. Sometimes it is used a variation of IOB tagging in order to simply merge the words at the beginning of the chink and the words within of the chunk. You will have to convert your nltk tree into IOB format.

```python
from nltk . chunk import conlltags2tree, tree2conlltags

sentence = " John and Lisa are working at Google. "

ne _ tree = ne _ chunk ( pos _ tag ( word _ tokenize ( sentence )))

iob _ tagged = tree2conlltags ( ne _ tree )

print iob _ tagged """ [( 'John', 'NNP', u'B-PERSON'), ( 'and', 'CC', u'O' ), ( 'John', 'NNP', u'B-PERSON' ), ( 'are', 'VBP', u'O' ), ( 'working', 'VBG', u'O' ), ( 'at', 'IN', u'O' ), ( 'Google', 'NNP', u'B-ORGANIZATION' ), ( '.', '.', u'O' )] """


ne _ tree = conlltags2tree ( iob_tagged )

print ne _ tree """ ( S (PERSON John/NNP) and/CC ( PERSON Lisa/ NNP) are/ VBP working/ VBG at/ IN ( ORGANIZATION Google/NNP ) ./.) """
```

It should be noted that NLTK does not have that proper English corpus when it comes to the named entity extraction. It has only corpuses for Dutch and Spanish. You can easily try that method that will be presented here since NLTK provides an amazing corpus for readers.

In this section, we will go with GMB or Groningen Meaning Bank. It is fairly large corpus containing a huge number of annotations, but it is not perfect. It is not gold when it comes to the standard corpuses since it is not entirely human annotated, so it is not considered to be a hundred percent correct. This corpus is mainly created using some already existing annotators notably converted by humans where required. In order to start, you will download the 2.2.0 version of this corpus.

As soon as you are done, you will see that this corpus is composed of an amazingly large amount of files in tags file. It will look very messy to you, but, in fact, the data is pretty structured. You will notice that a downloaded file will contain more different sentences that are separated by two newline characters. It should be noted that for every sentence, each word would be separated by one newline character. In addition, for each word, every annotation will be separated by a certain tab character.

```
import os

import collections

ner _ tags = collections . Counter ()

corpus _ root = " gmb-2.2.0 "

filename . endswith ( ".tags" )

file _ content = file _ handle . read () . decode( 'utf-8' ) . strip ()
```

```
annotated _ sentences = file _ content . split ( '\n\n' )

annotated _ tokens = [ seq for seq in annotated _ sentence
. split ( '\n' ) if seq]

standard _ form _ tokens = []

annotations = annotated _ token . split ('\t')

ner _ tags [ ner ] += 1

print ner _ tags
```

""" Counter ({ u'O': 1146068, u'geo-nam': 58388, u'org-nam': 48034, u'per-nam': 23790, u'gpe-nam': 20680, u'tim-dat': 12786, u'tim-dow': 11404, u'per-tit': 9800, u'per-fam': 8152, u'tim-yoc': 5290, u'tim-moy': 4262, u'per-giv': 2413, u'tim-clo': 891, u'art-nam': 866, u'eve-nam': 602, u'nat-nam': 300, u'tim-nam': 146, u'eve-ord': 107, u'per-ini': 60, u'org-leg': 60, u'per-ord': 38, u'tim-dom': 10, u'per-mid': 1, u'art-add': 1 }) """

It should be noted that you have to make sure that your set is that proper path to that unzipped corpus. Further, you will split your sentences as well as annotations. The following step is to interpret your tags a little bit. You will notice the composition of your tags as complete tags and sub-tags. Therefore you have org tag suitable for an organization, time for time indicator, per is equal to a person, geo is equal to a geographical entity, art equals artifact, eve corresponds to an event and not equals to some natural phenomenon. It should be noted that these sub-categories are greatly polluted so they are, in fact, unnecessary. In the following step, we will remove those sub-categories in order to focus only on main categories. In order to do so, you have to modify the code a little bit.

```
ner _ tags = collections . Counter ()

filename . endswith ( ".tags" )

file _ content = file _ handle . read () . decode ( 'utf-8' ) . strip ()

annotated _ sentences = file _ content . split ( '\n\n' )

annotated _ tokens = [ seq for seq in annotated _ sentence . split ( '\n' )

standard _ form _ tokens = [ ]

annotations = annotated _ token . split ( '\t' )

ner = annotations [ 0 ], annotations [ 1 ], annotations [ 3 ]

ner != ' O '

ner = ner . split ( '-' ) [ 0 ]

ner _ tags [ ner ] += 1

print ner _ tags
```

Counter ({ u'O': 1146068, u'geo': 58388, u'org': 48094, u'per': 44254, u'tim': 34789, u'gpe': 20680, u'art': 867, u'eve': 709, u'nat': 300 })

print "Words=", sum (ner _ tags . values ())

Words= 1354149

You will notice that this looks much better and less polluted. You also have an option to drop that last few tags in the case when they are not well represented in the corpus.

Training Your System

When it comes to the training your system, we will use very similar approach to one commonly used for training a part-of-speech tagger. In order to begin, you have to import string and init that stemmer. The following step is to pad the sequence with certain placeholders and shift that index with two in order to accommodate the padding. This feature extraction will work just like features working as the part of part-of-speech tagger training except for added history mechanism. It should be noted that IOB tag is an amazingly good indicator or what your current IOB tag will be, so you will include that previous IOB tag as a mean feature.

```python
import string

from nltk . stem . snowball import SnowballStemmer

def features ( tokens, index, history ):
    """ `tokens` = a POS-tagged sentence [( w1, t1 ), ...]
    `index` = the index of the token we want to extract
    features for

    `history` = the previous predicted IOB tags """
    stemmer = SnowballStemmer ( 'english' )

    tokens = [( '[ START2 ]', '[START2]'), ('[ START1 ]', '[
    START1 ]')] + list ( tokens ) + [('[ END1 ]', '[ END1 ]'), ('[
    END2 ]', '[END2 ]')]

    history = ['[ START2 ]', '[ START1 ]'] + list ( history )
    index += 2 word
    pos = tokens [ index ]
    prevword, prevpos = tokens [ index – 1 ]
    prevprevword, prevprevpos = tokens [ index – 2 ]
    nextword, nextpos = tokens [ index + 1 ]
    nextnextword, nextnextpos = tokens [ index + 2 ]
    previob = history [ index – 1 ]
    contains _ dash = '-' in word
```

contains _ dot = '.' in word

allascii = all ([True for c in word if c in string . ascii _ lowercase])

allcaps = word = = word . capitalize ()

capitalized = word [0] in string . ascii _ uppercase

prevallcaps = prevword = = prevword . capitalize ()

prevcapitalized = prevword [0] in string . ascii _ uppercase

nextallcaps = prevword = = prevword . capitalize ()

nextcapitalized = prevword [0] in string . ascii _ uppercase

return

{ 'word': word, 'lemma': stemmer . stem (word),

'pos': pos,

'all - ascii': allascii,

'next - word': nextword,

'next - lemma': stemmer . stem (nextword),

'next - pos': nextpos,

'next – next - word': nextnextword,

'nextnextpos': nextnextpos,

'prev - word': prevword,

'prev - lemma': stemmer . stem (prevword),

'prev - pos': prevpos,

'prev - prev - word': prevprevword,

'prev – prev - pos': prevprevpos,

'prev-iob': previob,

'contains-dash': contains _ dash,

'contains-dot': contains _ dot,

'all - caps': allcaps,

'capitalized': capitalized,

'prev – all - caps': prevallcaps,

'prev-capitalized': prevcapitalized,

'next – all - caps': nextallcaps,

'next - capitalized': nextcapitalized, }

The following step is to create the utility functions in order to make the training process easier as well as to move that corpus reading stuff into a certain read gmb function. You will manage to read your sentences from that corpus in some proper format. The following step is to actually start training your system and NLTK provides an amazing amount of very helpful classes in order to help you train your system. You will use a Naive Bayes classifier in order to predict certain sequences.

```python
def to _ conll _ iob ( annotated _ sentence )

proper _ iob _ tokens = [ ]

ner = annotated _ token

ner != ' O '

idx = = 0:

ner = "B-" + ner elif annotated _ sentence [ idx – 1 ] [ 2 ]
= = ner

ner = "I-" + ner

ner = "B-" + ner

proper _ iob _ tokens . append (( tag, word, ner ))

return proper _ iob _ tokens

def read _ gmb ( corpus _ root )

filename . endswith ( ".tags" )

file _ content = file _ handle . read ( ) . decode ( 'utf-8' ) .
strip ( )

annotated _ sentences = file _ content . split ( '\n\n' )

annotated _ tokens = [ seq for seq in annotated _ sentence
. split ( '\n' ) if seq ]

standard _ form _ tokens = [ ]

annotations = annotated _ token . split ( '\t' )

ner = annotations [ 0 ], annotations [ 1 ], annotations [ 3 ]
```

```
ner != 'O':

ner = ner . split ( '-' ) [ 0 ]

tag = "``"

standard _ form _ tokens . append (( word, tag, ner ))

conll _ tokens = to _ conll _ iob ( standard _ form _
tokens )

yield [(( w, t ), iob ) for w, t, iob in conll _ tokens ]

reader = read _ gmb ( corpus _ root )
```

When it comes to the training your system, you will use a certain annotated sentence containing a list of triplets including person and location. The following step is to make your NLTK entirely compatible to that NLTK classifier since the classifiers will expect a tuple to be the initial item input. As soon as you done, you will, check the output and you will see that you are able to read your sentences from your corpus easily in a proper format. In the following steps, you will transform your results to some preferred list containing triplet format. The next step is to transform that list containing triplets into NLTK.

```
import pickle

from collections import Iterable
```

```python
from nltk . tag import ClassifierBasedTagger

from nltk . chunk import ChunkParserI

class NamedEntityChunker ( ChunkParserI )

def __ init __ ( self, train _ sents, **kwargs )

assert isinstance ( train _ sents, Iterable )

self . feature _ detector = features

self.tagger = ClassifierBasedTagger ( train=train _ sents,
feature _ detector=features, **kwargs )

chunks = self . tagger . tag ( tagged _ sent )

iob _ triplets = [ ( w, t, c ) for ( ( w, t ), c ) in chunks ]

return conlltags2tree ( iob _ triplets )
```

The following step is to build the dataset, so your system will be able to recognize different named entities like in this case time and geographical entity. You also can test your system since you followed this good pattern in NLTK.

Chapter 3 Getting Started with NLTK

It is very easy to get your hands on millions of words contained in textual format. So, you wonder what can you do with that. You have numerous options available by combining simple programming techniques using Python that can easily handle large portions of unstructured text. You can automatically extract some keywords as well as various phrases notably summing the content and style of the text you have obtained. Python provides many different tools and kits in order to perform such action like Natural Language Processing kit or simply NLTK. In this section of the book, you will get to know NLTK and the concept behind it. You will use some raw data for your program that will manipulate that data in a variety of different as well as exciting ways. Before you embark on this adventure, you have to get started with certain Python interpreter.

There are numerous friendly things about Python especially since it allows you to type some words directly into Python interactive interpreter. It is a certain programme that will run all of your Python programmes. You are able to access it using a very simple graphical interface IDLE or Interactive DeveLopment Environment. Under Unix, you are able to run it from the shell just by typing idle. As soon as you are don, the interpreter will print everything about your current Python version.

Python 3.4.2 (default, Oct 15 2014, 22:01:37)

[GCC 4.2.1 Compatible Apple LLVM 5.1 (clang-503.0.40)] on darwin

Type "help", "copyright", "credits" or "license" for more information

If you are unable to run the program, it is because you do not have Python installed at all. In order to get your Python version, just visit Python website, which provides all details about latest NLTK versions notably working excellently on the latest Python versions. In the case when you already installed the program, you will see that it automatically indicates the Python interpreter waiting for some new input. In order to test it, you can do some calculations so Python will be used as a calculator. As soon as you are done, you will see that the prompt reappear displaying your answer. In order to do some more calculations, you simply enter more expressions of your own using an asterisk and other commands. In the next section, you will see the preceding exampled notably demonstrating how you can work very interactively with this Python interpreter. You are able to experiment with various expressions in the language and you will see what the program will do with them.

In the case when you try some nonsensical expression, the Python interpreter will display a syntax error. In Python, it really does not make any sense if you end your expression with certain plus sign. The program will automatically indicate a certain line when the issue occurred. As soon as you are ready with NLTK, you are able to work with your language data. In order to start, you will install latest NLTK version and by following provided instructions, you will be ready in almost no time. Once you have your NLTK version, you will use the Python interpreter just like in the previous example. You will install all required data for your task and then type commands at the interpreter.

```
import nltk
nltk . download ()
from nltk.book import
Loading text1, ..., text9 and sent1, ..., sent9
Type the name of the text or sentence to view it
Type: 'texts ( )' or 'sents ( )' to list the materials.
text1: Moby Dick by Herman Melville 1851
```

text2: Sense and Sensibility by Jane Austen 1811

text3: Inaugural Address Corpus

text4: Chat Corpus

text5: Monty Python and the Holy Grail

text6: The Man Who Was Thursday by G . K . Chesterton 1908

Once all the required data is downloaded, you are able to load some data into the interpreter. The initial step is to type some special command at the prompt that tells the interpreter to load your text so you can further explore it using NLTK. You will use command from nltk import. This certain command tells the program to load certain textual data. The certain book module will contain all the data needed in order to process it further using the program. As soon as you start, you will see that welcome message and your text will be loaded. Make sure that you check your spelling and punctuation. Anytime you want to find out more about some textual data, you will type the names directly at the Python interpreter.

Searching Syntax

When it comes to the searching text or syntax in order to examine the content of your text, there are many ways to so, so you have options besides just reading your text. In order to display the content, you will use a concordance view notably showing you every occurrence of a certain word together with the context. For instance, you can search for a certain word in some book. In the following section, we will search for word monstrous in the Moby Dick book. In order to do so, you will enter text1 command followed by the term concordance. You will place word monstrous in the command like as well after you entered the word concordance. The very first time when you use this term concordance, the overall process may take up to few minutes since the program has to take some time in order to build a certain index containing your subsequent searches.

text1 . concordance("monstrous")

Displaying matches:

One was of a most monstrous size

Touching that monstrous bulk of the whale or ork

Heathenish array of monstrous clubs and spears

Some were thick d as you gazed, and wondered what monstrous cannibal and savage could ever have that has survived the flood

Most monstrous and most mountainous

In connection with the monstrous pictures of whales

I am strongly here to enter upon those still more monstrous stories of them

Out of this monstrous cabinet

Whales of a monstrous size...

You have an option to search for any word you like. When it comes to the saving your typing, you can use different commands in order to access your previous command in order to further modify the word that you have searched previously. You can try searches on some other books, articles and pretty much everything else that are included in NLTK and the process will be the same like in this previous example using command concordance. Once you have spent more time examining your text, you will get that sense of richness as well as that great diversity of language. This command concordance will allow you to see words in some context. You have an option to find out more by appending another term similar to that word you are searching.

text1 . similar ("monstrous")

text2 . similar ("monstrous")

You will notice that you got the different results when it comes to the different texts. You will notice that other words will appear in a very similar range of contexts and you will find those contexts by typing similar in the command line. Further, you will insert some relevant words that you are looking for in parentheses. You also have an option to use another term, common context notably allowing you to examine only a single context, which is shared by two or more words like very and monstrous. In order to do so, you will enclose your words in square brackets and further separate them using a comma.

text2.common _ contexts (["monstrous", "very"])

a _ pretty is _ pretty am _ glad be _ glad a _ lucky

You may pick another pair of words and further compare their usage in different texts using that common context and similar functions. These functions automatically will detect your particular word occurring in some obtained textual data. Further, it will display those words you have searched for and their occurrence within a certain context. This function also can easily determine the location of some word in the text. The function also may show you how many times that same word appears in some context. These location related information will be displayed using command dispersion plot. It will represent every stripe regarding the instance of a certain word while every row will represent the complete text. You are able to produce different plots using a dispersion plot displaying information regarding the location and position of the text. You can type various words and different texts, just make sure that you use brackets, quotes, parentheses, and commas correctly.

text4 . dispersion _ plot (["citizens", "democracy", "freedom", "liberty", "world"])

text3 . generate ( )

It should be noted that you would Matplotlib and NumPy packages are installed to produce some graphical plots. You also have an option to plot the frequency of some word through time. The last step when it comes to the searching syntax is to generate your text in the different styles. In order to do so, you will just enter the name of the text and add term generate. It should be noted that you have to include parentheses, but you will not separate them with commas.

Sentence Tokenization

NLTK is a leading platform when it comes to the natural language processing in Python. It is designed in order to work with human language while providing easy-to-use interface containing more than fifty corpora and different lexical resources like WordNet an addition to a suite of various text processing libraries used for classification, tagging, parsing, tokenization, semantic reasoning and everything else needed to embark on this text analytics journey.

NLTK has proven to be an amazing tool for working in and learning using Python containing an amazing library used to play with natural language. Thanks so very comprehensive API documentation and provided computational linguistics, educators, students, researchers, and analytics gladly use NLTK when it comes to the text analytics tasks. Due to these numerous advantages, we will use NLTK in order to tokenize text and words. We will use NLTK tokenizer that will divide a string into some sub-strings by dividing that specified string. In lexical meaning, it is a lexical analysis of textual content meaning you will be splitting your text into a sentence. Even though it seems like a very simple task, it may be challenging.

NLTK tokenizer is designed in order to be very flexible as well as very easy to adapt to some new domains and challenging tasks. The concept lying behind simple NLTK tokenizer is that tuple regex string notably defining a list of some regular expression strings. These strings are into certain order containing a compiled list of various regular expression objects we call words.

The overall process of tokenization will be performed using certain word re-findall. In this situation, the letter S corresponds to the certain user-supplied string contained inside that certain tokenizer. When you are installing tokenizer objects, you will have a single command known as preserve case. By default, this option is set to be True. On the other hand, if you set it to be false, your tokenizer immediately down-case everything but emoticons.

span _ tokenize (s) [source]

tokenize (s)

You have an option to use this tokenizer feature for Tweets called as Tweet Tokenizer. You will use the base set as different objects by preserve case command that will set as default True. The first step is to import Tweet Tokenizer.

```
from nltk . tokenize import TweetTokenizer

tknzr = TweetTokenizer ( )

s0 = " This is a cooool # dummysmiley: :-) :-P <3 and
some arrows < > -> <--"

tknzr . tokenize (s0) [ ' This ', ' is ', ' a ', ' cooool ', '#
dummysmiley', ':', ':-)', ':-P', '<3', 'and', 'some', 'arrows']

tknzr = TweetTokenizer ( strip _ handles = True, reduce _
len=True )

s1 = '@remy: This is way too much for you!!!!!!'

tknzr . tokenize ( s1 ) [ ':', 'This', 'is', 'way', 'too', 'much',
'for', 'you', '!', '!', '!']
```

When it comes to the parameters that you will use, the first
one is text and return command. Returns parameter
represents a tokenized list of different strings. This list will
be returned to that original list if you use command preserve
case and set it to False. You will also use convenience
function when it comes to the wrapping your tokenizer. By
lexical analysis or sentence tokenization, you will convert a
sequence of different characters contained in textual format
into certain sequences of tokens. These tokens represent
certain strings that come with already assigned and
identified meaning. The program used for sentence

tokenization, in this case, NLTK will analyze the syntax of textual data.

We will use sentence tokenizer in order to find a certain list of various sentences. You can also find different Word tokenizer that you can further use in order to find strings contained in certain words. Tokenizing text into specific sentences is also known as sentence segmentation, sentence boundary disambiguation or sentence boundary detection known as sentence-breaking.

Sentence boundary disambiguation or sentence breaking is among the main problems when it comes to the natural language processing. It is the process of deciding where certain sentences begin and where they end. It is common for natural language processing tools to require their input to be previously divided into certain sentences for many reasons.

On the other hand, sentence boundary disambiguation is very challenging since punctuation marks are greatly ambiguous. For instance, a period may denote decimal point or abbreviation, but not the end of a sentence. There are many tools available when it comes to the sentence tokenization like NLTK, which will use. In order to begin, you will install nltk data and launch the program. You will import sentence tokenization tool from NLTK.

text = this's a sent tokenize test.

from nltk . tokenize import sent _ tokenize

sent _ tokenize _ list = sent _ tokenize (text)

len (sent _ tokenize _ list)

sent _ tokenize _ list [" this's a sent tokenize test. "]

You will use a sent tokenize test after you have imported from NLTK tokenization tool. You will use command sent tokenize from the NLTK. It should be noted that this instance has already been trained and it will work for almost every European language. It already knows what characters and punctuation marks end sentences and what the beginning of a new sentence looks like. You will use sent command sent tokenize of Punkt Sentence Tokenizer from that nltk tokenize command. It should be noted that this Tokenize Punkt has been already trained model used for the majority of European languages. There are seventeen languages supported by NLTK when it comes to the sentence tokenization, and you are able of using all of them.

```
import nltk . data
```

```
tokenizer = nltk . data . load ( ' tokenizers / punkt
/English . pickle' )
```

```
tokenizer . tokenize ( text ) [ "this's a sent tokenize test." , '
this is sent two.' , 'is this sent three?' , ']
```

A spanish sentence tokenize example:

```
spanish _ tokenizer = nltk . data . load ( ' tokenizers/
punkt/ spanish . pickle' )
```

```
spanish _ tokenizer . tokenize ( 'Hola amigo. Estoy bien.' )
[ 'Hola amigo.', 'Estoy bien.' ]
```

When it comes to the tokenizing some text into word using Python's NLTK, the process is very simple. You will only have to use command word tokenize from that previous nltk tokenize module. It should be noted that this command word tokenizer, in fact, is a simple wrapper function notably calling tokenize.

```
from nltk . tokenize import word _ tokenize
```

```
word _ tokenize ( ' Hello World. ' ) [ ' Hello ', ' World ', '.' ]
```

```
word _ tokenize ( " this's a test " ) [ ' this ', " 's ", ' a ', 'test' ]
```

Standard word tokenizer:

```
_word _ tokenize = TreebankWordTokenizer ( ) . tokenize
```

```
def word _ tokenize ( text )

return _ word _ tokenize( text )
```

In this example, you have seen that standard work tokenizer just returns that tokenized copy of your text since it is designed in order to work on a single sentence at a time. However, there is another equivalent method you can use in order to provide the same result. You also have an option to use different word tokenizers in addition to what I have used here Word Punkt Tokenizer. You may use Punkt Tokenizer that splits on punctuation but at the same time keeps it within the word.

```
from nltk . tokenize import TreebankWordTokenizer

tokenizer = TreebankWordTokenizer ( )

tokenizer . tokenize ( " this's a test " ) [ ' this ', "" s ", ' a ', ' test ' ]

from nltk . tokenize import PunktWordTokenizer

punkt _ word _ tokenizer = PunktWordTokenizer ( )

punkt _ word _ tokenizer . tokenize ( " this's a test " ) [ ' this ', "" s ", ' a ', ' test ' ]
```

You have an option to choose any word tokenizer your like from NLTK depending on your using purpose. In the following chapter, you will how to use NLTK in order to automatically summarize any text you have obtained.

Chapter 4 Automatic Text Summarization

Automatic text summarization is common text analytics process of reducing some text document using a computer program to create a summary, which will retain only the most important points of that original document. Since there is a common problem when it comes to the overloading of information since it has grown rapidly, the quantity of data has rapidly increased. Therefore, we simply need a program that will perform an automatic text summarization. Fortunately, technologies available can easily make that coherent summary taking into account different variables like writing style, syntax, and length of some text document. In order to start, you will import NLTK summarizer.

```
from summa import summarizer

print summarizer . summarize ( text )
```

The next step is to extract keywords. Like I already stated , text summarization process is all about generating summaries from some given long text. We will use an approach of extracting sentences, which consist of some more frequent words, so the overall process of text summarization may be easily performed just by extracting a few certain sentences.


```
from nltk . tokenize import sent _ tokenize, word _
tokenize

from nltk . corpus import stopwords

from collections import defaultdict

from string import punctuation

from heapq import nlargest

class Summarize _ Frequency: def __ init __ ( self, cut _
min=0.2, cut _ max=0.8):
```


You will use function class summarize frequency and then you will initialize certain text summarizer. It should be noted that words, which have certain frequency term lower than function cut min or higher than function cut max will be entirely ignored. When it comes to the keyword extraction, you will use function print keywords.


```
from summa import keywords

print keywords . keywords ( text )
```


Your installed software will depend on Scipy and NumPy, two packages commonly used for scientific computing. It should be noted that you have to install them before you begin a process of text summarization. If you are going to use a certain export function, then you will install NeworkX, so you will install Pattern in order to enhance keyword extraction process. In the following section, you will learn how to use command-line, how to export and how to define the length of your summary corresponding to a certain proportion of your text which is also available in keywords.

```
cd path/ to/ folder/ summa/ python textrank.py -t FILE
from summa . export import gexf _ export
gexf _ export ( text, path = "graph . gexf " )
from summa . summarizer import summarize
summarize ( text, ratio = 0.2 )
summarize ( text, words=50 )
summarize ( text, language = 'spanish' )
summarize ( text, split = True )
```

You also have an option to summarize your text by defining a length of your summary using an approximate number of contained words. You also have to define the input language available in keywords. The final step is to get your results using summarize function.

Chapter 5 Text Classification Using Scikit-Learn and NLTK

In this chapter, you will get to know how to use popular Python library scikit-learn in order to classify certain text. It should be noted that document text classification is one of the most important as well as the most common task when it comes to the text analytics tasks. Assigning certain categories to textual data that can be a library book, web page, gallery or media articles has various applications like email routing, spam filtering, and sentiment analysis.

Before you embark on text classification using Python's scikit-learn we will divide this task into certain steps. The first step will be to set up a certain environment and load the relevant data set in jupyter. The following step requires extracting useful features from your text files and running ML models. The next step includes Grid Search in order to perform parameter tuning.

For your first step of setting up a certain environment, you will have to provide Python version 2.7.3. in addition to the jupyter notebook. You will have to install anaconda. It will not be a problem to execute this test since you already know the fundamentals behind text analytics. For text classification, you will use scikit-learn in addition to a little bit of NLTK. The second step includes loading the data set, and for this step, you can use any set you previously obtained.

In this section, I will show you how to use 20 Newsgroup data collection containing around 20,000 newsgroup documents notably partitioned evenly across twenty different newsgroups. This certain collection was introduced by Ken Lang. It has become very popular data set when it comes to the various text analytics experiments using various machine learning techniques like text clustering and text classification.

It should be noted that this data collection is already built in scikit-learn, so you can begin immediately. You will open a command prompt and just type jupyter notebook. Further, you will open the notebook and your session will immediately start. You will select Python 2 and give a certain name to the obtained jupyter notebook. The next step is to load the data collection which will take up to few minutes.

```
from sklearn . datasets import fetch _ 20newsgroups

twenty _ train = fetch _ 20newsgroups ( subset= ' train ',
shuffle = True )
```

It should be noted that you will load the test data entirely separate from the training data. The next step requires checking the categoric or target named and data files and you will print all available categories while using command notably printing an initial line of your first data file.

twenty _ train . target _ names

print (" \ n " . join (twenty _ train . data [0] . split (" \ n ") [:3]))

The following step requires extracting valuable features from your text file. A text file is only series containing words in order and to run machine learning model you will have to convert a certain text file into specific numerical feature vectors. In this case, you will use a bag of words algorithm. As soon as you obtain the bag of words, you will segment every text file into certain words splitting them using space. You also have to count how many times every word occurs in every text document and then you will assign every word an integer. It should be noted that every word contained in your dictionary will correspond to certain descriptive feature. Fortunately, scikit-learn has a very high-level component that will easily create all required feature vectors using Count Vectorizer.

```
from sklearn . feature _ extraction . text import
CountVectorizer

count _ vect = CountVectorizer ( )
X _ train _ counts = count _ vect . fit _ transform ( twenty
_ train . data )
X _ train _ counts . shape
```

In this previous example by using count vector and fit transform function, you will be learning certain vocabulary dictionary notably returning your document's matrices. Further, you have to use function term frequencies that just counts the number of every word in every document since there is an issue. It will give greater weigh the to some longer documents. In order to avoid this issue, you will use term frequencies that count a total number of words in every document. The final step requires reducing that weight of some very common words like an, is or the. This generally is called as term frequency times inverse total document frequency.

```
from sklearn . feature _ extraction . text
import TfidfTransformer
tfidf _ transformer = TfidfTransformer ( )
X _ train _ tfidf = tfidf _ transformer . fit _ transform ( X
_ train _ counts )
X _ train _ tfidf . shape
```

The following step required in any text classification task is running ML models. There are various models that can be used for text classification task. In this case, I will use a single Naive Bayes notably the simplest one. You can very easily build a Naive Bayes classifier using Python's scikit-learn with just two lines of codes. As soon as you are done, you will have to train your Naive Bayer classifier on your training data and then build a pipeline.

```
from sklearn . naive _ bayes import MultinomialNB
clf = MultinomialNB ( ) . fit ( X _ train _ tfidf, twenty _
train . target )
from sklearn . pipeline import Pipeline
text _ clf = Pipeline ( [ (' vect ', CountVectorizer ( ) ), ...
( 'tfidf', TfidfTransformer ( ) ), ...
( 'clf', MultinomialNB ( ) ), ... ] )
```

text _ clf = text _ clf . fit (twenty _ train . data, twenty _ train . target)

It should be noted that arbitrary vectors will be used in the following steps. The next step is to calculate the overall performance of your Naive Bayer classifier on your test set. You will get an approximate accuracy and if it is above seventy percent, then consider your Naive Bayes properly working since that accuracy is not bad at all for a Naive classifier. Then, you will have to use SVMs or support vector machines if you want to check your model and try getting some better performance results. You will see that you performance accuracy is better while using support vector machines. It will probably be above eighty percent.

import numpy as np

twenty _ test = fetch _ 20newsgroups (subset =' test ', shuffle = True)

predicted = text _ clf . predict (twenty _ test . data)

np . mean (predicted = = twenty _ test . target)

from sklearn . linear _ model import SGDClassifier

text _ clf _ svm = Pipeline ([('vect' , CountVectorizer ( ))

('tfidf', TfidfTransformer ( ))

```
( 'clf-svm', SGDClassifier ( loss = ' hinge ', penalty = ' l2 ',
... alpha = 1e - 3, n _ iter = 5, random _ state = 42 ) ), ... ] )
```

```
_ = text _ clf _ svm . fit ( twenty _ train . data, twenty _
train . target )
```

```
predicted _ svm = text _ clf _ svm . predict ( twenty _ test
. data )
```

```
np . mean ( predicted _ svm = = twenty _ test . target )
```

Like I already mentioned, the last step in this text classification task is grid search. It should be noted that almost every classifier will contain various parameters which easily can be tuned in order to obtain that optimal performance. Python's scikit-learn when it comes to the Grid Search is an extremely useful tool. You will create a certain list containing different parameters notably used in order to tune the overall performance of your model. Every parameters name will start with certain classifier name. The next step required is creating an instance of that grid search by passing certain classifiers and parameters. In order to do so, you will use function n jobs that tell your model to use some multiple cores from your model.

```
from sklearn . model _ selection import GridSearchCV
```

```
parameters = {'vect __ ngram _ range ' : [( 1, 1 ), ( 1, 2 )],
...

'tfidf __ use _ idf ': ( True, False ), ...

'clf __ alpha': ( 1e-2, 1e-3 ),...

gs _ clf = GridSearchCV ( text _ clf, parameters, n _ jobs=
- 1 )

gs _ clf = gs_clf.fit(twenty_train.data, twenty _ train .
target )

gs _ clf . best _ score _ gs _ clf . best _ params _
```

It should be noted that this process will take a few minutes depending on your machine configuration. The last step is to see that best mean score in addition to the params. You will notice that you have increased your overall model's performance up to ninety percent for your Naive Bayes classifier. Very similarly you can improve the overall performance of your support vector machine classifier in the same manner by tuning relevant parameters.

```
from sklearn . model _ selection import GridSearchCV

parameters _ svm = { ' vect __ ngram _ range ' : [ ( 1, 1 ), (
1, 2 ) ], ...

'tfidf __ use _ idf ': ( True, False ), ...
```

```python
from nltk . stem . snowball import SnowballStemmer

stemmer = SnowballStemmer ( " english ", ignore _
stopwords = True )

class StemmedCountVectorizer ( CountVectorizer )

analyzer = super ( StemmedCountVectorizer, self ) . build
_ analyzer ( )

return lambda doc:

( [ stemmer . stem ( w ) for w in analyzer ( doc ) ] )

stemmed _ count _ vect = StemmedCountVectorizer (
stop _ words = ' english ' )

text _ mnb_stemmed = Pipeline ( [ ( ' vect ', stemmed _
count _ vect ), ...

( ' tfidf ', TfidfTransformer ( ) ), ...

( ' mnb ', MultinomialNB ( fit _ prior = False ) ), ... ] )

text _ mnb _ stemmed = text _ mnb _ stemmed . fit (
twenty _ train . data, twenty _ train . target )

predicted _ mnb _ stemmed = text _ mnb _ stemmed .
predict ( twenty _ test . data )

np . mean ( predicted _ mnb _ stemmed = = twenty _ test
. target )
```

Using NLTK Snowball stemmer, you will be able to improve your model's accuracy up to eighty-two percent even though it will be only a marginal improvement with Naive Bayes classifier. You can use word stemmer on your other algorithms as well like support vector machines. In this chapter, you have seen how to perform text or document classification using Python's NLTK and scikit-learn. Now, you also know what can greatly improve your model's accuracy especially if you use already built-in word stemmer in NTLK. You have also seen that for your data set, both of these two used algorithms equally matched while being optimized. Commonly when you have enough data set, that certain choice of different algorithms will not make any significant difference.

Topic Modeling

When it comes to the analytics industry and text analytics in generall, it is all about obtaining some useful information from some unstructured data. We all have witnessed that rapidly growing amount of data especially when it comes to these recent years. Fortunately, technology has provided and developed some very powerful techniques that can be easily used in order to mine through the data and further fetch the information that is useful and relevant and something we are looking for.

One very useful text analytics technique is topic modeling. It is commonly used process in order to automatically identify some topics notably present in some text object. Topic modeling process further derives that hidden patterns notably exhibited by some text corpus.

Topic modeling is greatly different from some rule-based text analytics techniques which use those regular expressions as well as some dictionary based keyword techniques. It should be noted that this process is an unsupervised method commonly used for finding as well as observing some bunch of words namely topics in a certain large cluster of textual data. These topics are commonly defined as some repeating pattern of that co-occurring terms in a certain text corpus.

Topic models come to be very useful for various text analytics purposes like organizing some large blocks of various textual data, document clustering, feature selection or information retrieval. For instance, some major publishing companies like New York Times are using text analytics topic models in order to boost their article recommendations systems.

On the other hand, various other professionals turn to topic modeling when it comes to the recruitment industries where they mainly aim to extract those latent features of various job descriptions a and to further map them to those right candidates. Topic models are commonly used when it comes to the organizing some large datasets like customer reviews, social media profiles or emails.

When it comes to the obtaining topics from some textual data, you can use several approaches including inverse document frequency and term frequency. However, the most popular technique used in topic modeling is Latent Dirichlet Allocation since it assumes various documents notably produced from a certain mixture of different topics. These certain topics further are generated commonly based on certain probability distribution. This approach further backtracks as well as trie to figure certain topic from obtained textual data. The approach, in fact, is a matrix factorization technique using certain vector space or any collection of documents that can be easily represented as a certain document-term matrix.

When it comes to the parameters used in Latent Dirichlet Allocation, alpha parameter represents document-topic density while beta parameter represents that topic-word density. It should be noted that higher alpha parameter means that your document is composed of a greater number of topics while a lower value of alpha means that your document is composed of the lower amount of different topics. On the other hand, if you have beta parameter higher your document contains a higher amount of words while lower beta parameter means that your document is composed of the lower amount of words.

In the following section, you will estimate the number of topics, number of certain topic terms and number of specific passes or iterations. This number of a topic will be directly extracted from your obtained corpus while a number of terms will be composed of a single topic. A number of iterations or passes will give you that maximum number of all allowed passes to your Latent Dirichlet Allocation for further convergence. In order to begin, you will import some sample documents in order to form your text corpus.

doc1 = " "

doc2 = " "

doc3 = " "

doc4 = " "

```
doc5 = " "

doc_complete = [ doc1, doc2, doc3, doc4, doc5 ]
```

The next step is data preprocessing and data cleaning. These two steps are among the most important steps when it comes to the topic modeling where you will remove the stopwords and punctuations in order to normalize your corpus. In this step, we will use again NLTK.

```
from nltk . corpus import stopwords

from nltk . stem . wordnet import WordNetLemmatizer

import string

stop = set ( stopwords . words ( ' english ' ) )

exclude = set ( string . punctuation )

lemma = WordNetLemmatizer ( )

def clean ( doc ):

stop _ free = " ". join ( [ i for i in doc . lower ( ) . split ( ) if
i not in stop ] )

punc _ free = " . join (ch for ch in stop _ free if ch not in
exclude )

normalized = " " . join ( lemma . lemmatize ( word ) for
word in punc _ free. split ( ) )
```

return normalized doc _ clean = [clean (doc) . split ( ) for doc in doc _ complete]

The following step requires preparing your document-term matrix. You already know that all obtained documents combined will for a corpus. In order to run mathematical models on your text corpus, you will convert it into certain matrix representation. Python provides amazing libraries when it comes to the text analytics practices like gensim. As soon as you import library gensim, you will create that term dictionary of your corpus where every since term will be assigned an index. The next step is to convert your list of documents into a certain document-term matrix.

```
import gensim

from gensim import corpora

index . dictionary = corpora . Dictionary ( doc _ clean )

doc _ term _ matrix = [ dictionary . doc2bow ( doc ) for doc in doc _ clean ]
```

The following step of topic modeling requires running your Latent Dirichlet Allocation model. You will train your model on your document-term matrix. It should be noted that this training will require a few parameters like input.

The gensim module will allow you both your model estimation from an inference of topic distribution and from training model on some new and unseen documents.

Lda = gensim . models . ldamodel . LdaModel

ldamodel = Lda (doc _ term _ matrix, num _ topics = 3, id2word = dictionary, passes = 50)

print (ldamodel . print _ topics (num _ topics = 3, num _ words = 3)) ['0.168* + 0.083* + 0.072*, '0.061* + 0.050* + 0.050*, '0.049* + 0.049* + 0.049*]

It should be noted that every line is a certain topic within some individual weights and topic terms. Also, these results of your topic models are entirely dependant on some terms or features notably present in your corpus. Your corpus is represented entirely as document term matrix that is very spared in its nature. On the other hand, if you reduce the overall dimensionality of the matrix, you will be able to greatly improve the results of your topic modeling process. I order to do so, you can turn to frequency filter, part of speech tag filter or batch-wise LDA.

If you use frequency filter, you will arrange each term in accordance with its frequency. It should be noted that terms with some higher frequencies have a greater probability of appearing in your results as those with some lower frequencies. Also, these low-frequency terms are weak features within your corpus, so it is a great approach if you just get rid of all weak features using exploratory analysis of different teams notably helping you decide what certain frequency value may be considered as that specific threshold.

You also can use batch wise LDA to retrieve some of the most important topic terms. If you use this feature, you will divide your corpus into certain batches of some fixed sizes. If you run LDA multiple times on these specific batches, you will generate different results. It should be noted that the best batch wise LDA approach is to do the intersection of all available batches. Also, model LDA commonly is used as valuable feature selection methods especially when you have complex text analytics task where your training data contains a greater number of wise documents.

Chapter 6 Part of Speech Tagging

Part of speech tagging is among the most important text analytics tasks commonly used when it comes to the classifying various words into their specific part-of-speech. This process also labels certain words in accordance to certain tagset that is a collection containing various tags commonly used for the part-of-speech tagging. This process is also commonly known as lexical or word classes. POS tagging is called grammatical tagging as well as word-category disambiguation.

The process includes making up various words in some corpus in correspondence to certain particular part of speech mainly based on its context and its definition. Once performed, POS tagging is entirely done in the certain context of specific computational linguistics using different modes that commonly associated with certain discrete terms also including specific hidden parts of speech according to a collection of various disruptive tags. It should be noted that POS-tagging models commonly fall into two different groups including stochastic and rule-based group. In the following section, you will get to know how to use POS tagging in Python's NLTK. In order to begin, you have to import certain Python interpreter using function word tokenizer just before pos tagging.

import nltk

text = nltk . word _ tokenize (" Dive into NLTK: Part – of - speech tagging and POS Tagger ") text [' Dive', 'into', 'NLTK', ':', 'Part – of - speech', ' tagging', ' and ', ' POS ', ' Tagger ']

nltk . pos _ tag (text) [('Dive', 'JJ'), ('into', 'IN'), ('NLTK', 'NNP'), (':', ':'), ('Part – of - speech', 'JJ'), ('tagging', 'NN'), ('and', 'CC'), ('POS', 'NNP'), ('Tagger', 'NNP')]

Fortunately, NLTK provides a huge amount of documentation for every tag that you will be using as a tag. The following step is to open NLTK help or some regular expression.

nltk . help . upenn _ tagset ('JJ')

nltk . help . upenn _ tagset ('IN')

nltk . help . upenn _ tagset ('NNP')

It should be noted that NLTK also provides a perfect method for POS tagging. In order to begin you will use function batch pos tag.

nltk . batch _ pos _ tag ([[' this ', ' is ', ' batch ', ' tag ', ' test '], [' nltk ', ' is ', ' text ', 'analysis', ' tool ']]) [[(' this ', ' DT '), (' is ', ' VBZ '), (' batch ', 'NN'), (' tag ', ' NN '), (' test ', ' NN ')], [(' nltk ', ' NN '), (' is ', ' VBZ '), (' text ', ' JJ '), (' analysis ', ' NN '), (' tool ', ' NN ')]]

POS Tagging Model in NLTK

In this section, we will use NLTK already built-in POS tagging models. You can find all the needed code in maxent treebank pos tagging model. You will use standard treebank tagger. In this task, you will use that currently recommended part of NLTK POS tagging speech model in order to tag certain list of different tokens. Further, you will use the same model in order to tag sequence of tokens and to tag some given list of different sentences notably consisting of a collection of tokens.

POS _ TAGGER = ' taggers/ maxent _ treebank _ pos _ tagger/english . pickle'

```
def pos _ tag ( tokens )

from nltk . tag import pos _ tag # doctest: + SKIP

from nltk . tokenize import word _ tokenize # doctest: +
SKIP

pos _ tag ( word _ tokenize ( "Lisa's big idea # doctest:
+SKIP [(' Lisa ', ' NNP '), ("'s", ' PO S'), (' big ', ' JJ '), ('
idea ', ' NN '), (',',',') ]

tagger . tag ( tokens )

def batch _ pos _ tag ( sentences )

tagger = load ( _ POS _ TAGGER )

return tagger . batch _ tag ( sentences )
```

The following step is to train your POS model. In order to
do so, you will need to use the function maxent treebank
tagging model set by default. Fortunately, NLTK provides
this function in addition to other pos taggers like brill, CRF,
and TNT alongside different interfaces in addition to
Stanford pos tagging model, senna posttaggers and hunpos
pos tagging models. I order to train your model you will use
NLTK already built-in TnT tagger.

```
from __ future __ import print _ function

from math import log
```

```
from operator import itemgetter
```

```
from nltk . probability import FreqDist,
ConditionalFreqDist from nltk . tag . api import TaggerI
```

```
class TnT ( TaggerI )
```

It should be noted that it is possible to obtain that untrained POS tagger in order to create different tags for some unknown words using see init function. This function should be used only with certain sentence-delimited input since this tagger works the best when it is trained over some entirely sentence delimited input. On the other hand, it still produces proper results if the testing and training data are previously separated in all of the punctuation. It should be noted that your input for training data will be expected as a certain collection of sentences, and every sentence will be a certain list of tags, words, and tuples.

The following step is to train your test and train data. In order to do, you will use that already provided treebank data from NLTK's corpus. More specifically, you will use the initial 3000 treebank sentences as your train data while the rest of 914 sentences will be used as your test data. Further, you will train your POS tagger using train data in order to evaluate test data. The last step is to save your pos tagger model in pickle file. You are able to use is further any time you want.

Conclusion

Text analytics is all about converting some unstructured data into some meaningful data used for further analysis used commonly in order to measure various customer opinions, provide feedback or to entity modeling in order to support some mainly fact-based decision making. Text analytics techniques greatly help data analysis experts since these techniques are able of bridging that gap existing between marketer and analysts.

Advances in text analytics approach are common when it comes customer relationship and almost every other type of marketing industry. It helps marketers in order to organize as well as to classify that very confusing techniques while framing all the right questions. Further, text analytics helps marketer in order to find that successful meaning in almost every unstructured data notably helping them to develop some effective marketing strategies in better customer approach.

You already know that majority of data available to us is completely unstructured as well as text-heavy making it very challenging for data analysts to apply certain data wrangling in addition to visualization tools. However, using most common text analytics techniques those challenging tasks are things of past. If you are information professional, developer or if you are simply interested in creating and managing big data, this book will definitely help you on your journey.